The Wood In Winter

ex libris

Candlestick Press

Published by:
Candlestick Press,
Diversity House, 72 Nottingham Road,
Arnold, Nottingham NG5 6LF
www.candlestickpress.co.uk

Printed by Ratcliff & Roper Print Group, Nottinghamshire, UK

Donation to Woodland Trust
www.woodlandtrust.org.uk

ISBN 978 1 907598 42 5

Acknowledgements:
'Seven Words for Winter' by Nancy Campbell was first published in
Disko Bay, Enitharmon Press (2015) and Jackie Kay, 'Winter Heart', first
appeared in *Darling: New and Selected Poems*, Bloodaxe Books (2007).
Our thanks to both presses for their kind permission to reprint the
poems here.

Oh, if a tree could wander
and move with foot & wings!
It would not suffer the axe blows
and not the pain of saws!

For would the sun not wander
away in every night —
How could at every morning
the world be lighted up?

And if the ocean's water
would not rise to the sky,
How would the plants be quick-
ened

by streams and gentle rain?
The drop that left its homeland
the sea, and then returned —
It found an oyster waiting
And grew into a pearl.

Did Yusuf not leave his father
in grief and tears and despair?
Did he not by such a journey
gain kingdom and fortune white?
Did not the Prophet travel
to far Medina, friend?
And there he found a new king
and ruled a hundred lands.

You lack a foot to travel?
Then journey into yourself!
And like a mine of rubies
receive the sunbeams' print!
Out of yourself — such a journey
will lead you to your self,
It leads to transformation
of dust into pure gold!

— Rumi —

Love from

Daniel :)

Seven Words for Winter

ukiigatta last winter.
ukioq the winter; the whole year.
ukiukkut in winter; during the year.
ukiuuppaa the winter came upon her before she reached home, or finished building her house.
ukiorippoq she has a good winter; it is a good winter.
ukiorpoq the winter has come.
ukiortaaq the new year.

Nancy Campbell

The Wood In Winter

I stopped at the wood on my way home, lurching the Land Rover up on the verge. It was late for a winter afternoon, say around three.

My family used to own Pool Wood; to come back without authority was an awkward trespass.

The sky was off white.

To get into the wood from the lane I climbed over the iron field gate; this had galvanized the cold of centuries in its bars. Some rooks flew overhead; not the usual ragged, weary flight to roost, but an oaring deep and strong with their wings. They flew as straight as crows.

In the trees I felt safe from prying eyes, just another dark vertical shape among others: a human tree trunk. Anyway, no one comes looking for you in a wood.

I went to Pool Wood deliberately, so that I might find a certain thing. I followed the path hollowed into the pink clay by generations of badgers; it went on and on through the vast silence and the leafless trees. Their branches made for a perpetual wire cage overhead.

No birds sang. A solitary tree creeper searched an alder's bark, in much the same way a caretaker will check under the auditorium seats for rubbish after a concert.

God, life is hard for birds in winter. How dismal the jay's nest looked against the blank sky.

I reached the oak grove in rapidly descending dusk. Often oaks will keep their leaves until February. On that Christmas Eve the oaks were temple pillars of a lost civilization; they had no more botany than stone.

From one ivy clad ruin a wren, as small as a moth, peered at me. It was too feeble to tisk its default alarm.

At the fork in the path by the beech stand I did not haver, I went left. The other path, down through the dingle, ends in the year AD 01, or thereabouts. It is a path back through time because at its terminus are clumped three wild service trees. The trio of *sorbus torminalis* are a remnant of the original wildwood. Pool Wood existed when William conquered, it existed when the Romans trod their road to Hereford. Only brock has been resident longer.

The ground was bitter hard, and the previous night's frost had frozen-solid the usual toadstool smell of woodland. There was just the exhilarating purity of ice, a wipe-clean of the senses. But a strong rope of rank scent stretched across the path at one point – the odour of a vixen. Like brock, reynard is another ancient landowner. Humans never really own land, do they? It belongs to the eternal animals.

Rabbits had scratched at a pollarded alder, causing pale sores on its snaking raised roots.

Deep into the wood I startled a pheasant under briars. Or rather it startled me, racing headlong for take-off, wings whistling, eyes staring, beak shrieking. Feathers, caught in the bramble's barbs, fluttered up. Deer had been nibbling the briar's leaves, their habitual iron rations on days like these.

I began to hurry because of the shivering cold. I had forgotten my gloves.

We no longer fear winter like people did when their clothes were thin and they were forced to be out in the woods, gathering fuel, chopping trees, or as I had been earlier, tending sheep. Shakespeare mentions the fear of Samhain's cold over and over. In the poem 'Winter' he wrote:

> *When all about the wind doth blow*
> *And coughing drowns the parson's saw,*
> *And birds sit brooding in the snow*
> *And Marian's nose looks red and raw.*

And in King Lear, the haunting line of Edgar: 'Still through the hawthorn blows the cold wind'.

People claim they enjoy winter, but what they actually mean is they enjoy winter as a livener, a quick tease of the elements before resorting to their central heating. For anyone working outdoors, winter hurts.

The great empty trees, the solitude, the early falling gloom, bone-sticks snapping under rushing feet.

Then I reached the clearing, and there holding court in the centre was the lone holly tree. Just as always. And she - because berries only grow on female trees - was festooned with berries. Just as always.

It was a year of holly berry dearth. The Viking birds, the redwings and the fieldfares, had descended from the north and plundered all the other hollies for miles around.

The scarlet and the green of the holly was shockingly vivid on that midwinter afternoon. The holly was Queen of the Wood, arrayed in her finest. I had hardly dared hope she would still be standing, let alone bountiful with berries. It was over twenty years since I had last seen her.

Holly is the symbol of Christ, and was for centuries the physical mnemonic to remind us that 'Mary bore sweet Jesus Christ on Christmas Day in the morn' because its berries are red like His blood, its prickles ('sharp as any thorn') are akin to the Messiah's crown at crucifixion, and its leaves evergreen, an arboreal metaphor for eternal life.

Is the Nativity superstition? Perhaps, but my grandparents believed it, and so I was sent every Christmas Eve to get the holly from the tree in middle of Pool Wood. In summer my grandparents decked their house with hops, at yuletide with the holly and the ivy.

As a good grandson of the country, I do not care to be without holly at Christmas.

Lacking a knife, gingerly I tore off five sprigs of holly, though not carefully enough and shaving-spots of blood appeared on my hands. The berries were best lower down where the leaves were sharpest. But Nature always does pain with gain.

As boy and man my grandfather had gathered holly from the tree in the clearing. On that Christmas Eve I was his picture echo down the century.

It was as I turned to go that it started snowing. The snow was harsh, and shimmered noisily.

A wood on a winter's eve, no matter where you are, when the snow is falling through the trees, is existence stripped back to the elements. It is the Ice Age returned in miniature.

Snow makes everything old, including us, who stoop in its face. As I blundered along, shoulders hunched, my fingers laced through the holly sprigs for my house, I found something sitting before me on the path: the vixen, quite oblivious to the weather, and to me. Even through pelting snow and half-light her fur lustred. She burned alive.

The *red* fox. Then it struck me, red is the colour of the countryside in December; the fox, the holly berries, the huntsman's jacket, the robin singing over its winter territory.

The vixen screamed her mating call, which is the wail of all the bereaved, ever. If I had been cold before, I was colder then.

She howled again, and cocked her ears for a response. Nothing came back over the fields or through the trees and the swirl. We were only three or four yards apart. Something then alerted her - a sixth sense, a movement by me - and she turned and saw me: she was the very picture of wild grace against the snow.

A wood in a snowstorm at dusk belongs to the animals. With an airy disdain for my intrusion, she trotted away to be swallowed in the flailing white flakes.

Snow covers, and snow betrays. When I reached the edge of the wood by the lane, there were blue-shadow tracks in the snow. Three hares had crept from the stubble field into the lee of an ash tree.

And I saw that the velvet buds on the ash were fully formed, and full of promise.

Winter Heart

My love, the nights are coming now in the afternoons,
and it is nearly the time of year when everyone wonders
where they should be and with whom;
and you are in the room –

all full of heart on your face and your sleeve –
your lovely face open as the spring, in the winter
evening with the dark coming down like a good soul song –
'Darling, you send me, honest you do.'

So, maybe, stoke up the fire in the living room,
and light the long candles. Hold me close
while the stars outside shiver and spell out their names –
bright as any love, anywhere, any time.

Jackie Kay